# PRESSURE CANNING MEAT COOKBOOK

## A Comprehensive Guide to Pressure Canning Meat for Beginners

**BY PHOEBE SHELL**

## Table of Contents

# INTRODUCTION

Self-sufficiency goes together with canning and food preservation. And, for the main part, it's very clear and safe. If done correctly, canning is a valuable and safe technique for preserving food. The canning procedure involves putting items in jars and heating them to a level that kills bacteria that might cause illness or damage. Enzymes that might ruin the food are likewise inactivated by canning. During heating, the air is forced out of the jar, and when it cools, a vacuum seal is established. The vacuum seal stops air from entering the food and contaminates the food with bacteria.

Research-based canning practices must be adopted to properly home-can foods and avoid foodborne disease. Botulism is the most prevalent foodborne disease associated with household canned foods. From 1996 to 2014, the Centers for Disease Control and Prevention documented 210 botulism cases, with 145 of them connected to household-canned foods.

Foodborne diseases associated with household canned foods are frequently associated with the individual canning the items simply by not adopting evidence-based canning procedures, not utilizing pressure canners for low-acid foods, and disregarding indicators of spoiling, as well as an absence of information about botulism in domestically preserved foods.

Let's focus now on pressure canning.

Pressure canning is a household food storage method involving using specific facilities to prepare food at a greater temperature than the traditional water bath canning method. It's generally used to can meat and vegetables without high-acid additives.

Pressure canning is suitable for meat, seafood, poultry, soups, vegetables, and a mix of low and high-acid food. Because the technique renders these items shelf-stable, they may be used to manufacture homemade variants of canned vegetables and stocks available in the food section of the supermarket. Because you may pick the ingredients, the handmade version might be a more quality product than those sold in stores.

Let's get started if you are set to learn the ins and outs of canning meat.

# PRESERVATION AT HOME 101

Food preservation at home is still a prominent topic of discussion. When a shortage of canning supplies such as jars, lids, and canners became an actuality in 2020, experts and household food preservers noticed a surge in demand in home food preservation. As more people store food at home, it's worth revisiting the history of food preservation.

Although chemical reactions like oxidation can harm some food, most food is spoiled in-store by living organisms such as bacteria, molds, and yeast. As a result, food preservation methods rely on destroying or preventing the development of these microorganisms.

Many of our most popular methods of food preservation have been around since the dawn of time and can be found in a variety of places. Drying, smoking, pickling, and fermenting have all found their way into the cuisines of different nations worldwide. Although the approaches differ, they all aim to produce a condition that is unfriendly to microorganisms like molds, bacteria, and yeasts.

"Food starts to decay soon after it is harvested," stated the National Center for Home Food Preservation. Our forefathers had to figure out a technique to keep that food fresh over the winter months to eat. They froze meat on ice in cold climates and dry foods in sunlight in hot climates. The prehistoric man established roots and built communities because of these initial food preservation techniques. They didn't have to eat the kill or harvest right away, and they could save some for the future."

## ❖ Methods of Food Preservation

Drying is one of the ancient methods of preserving food. It's also one of the basics because it removes water, which prevents the growth of organisms. Meats, some fruits, and grains have all benefited from this method. Those familiar with drying food rarely use weight to judge whether a food is suitably dehydrated. Rather, they will assess the texture and look to determine whether it is dried. The main downside of this approach is that it alters the nature and flavor of the food, and it necessitates careful keeping once the drying process is finished. Because moisture can accumulate on the outside of dried foods, proper ventilation is required to prevent condensation. Mold can form on the base of the food; if there is any moisture on one, it can affect others, leading to spoilage of the entire food.

Before canning and refrigeration, many other methods of food preservation relied on naturally existing chemicals to slow the growth of spoilage-causing organisms. Meat and fish that have been smoked, for example, leave chemicals in the meat that kill microorganisms. By reducing the moisture level of the meat, smoking also helps to preserve it. Before smoking, meat is usually brined for a short time. Before being placed in the smoke, the meat is normally rinsed with lukewarm water and left to drain.

For smoking meat, many containers are utilized. Although a sealed box or barrel can be used, many farms operate a complete smokehouse for mass meat preservation. A typical structure has several hooks for holding food, a firebox to supply smoke, and tiny holes to allow smoke to escape the fire. The firebox is usually linked to the smokehouse via a tiny tunnel to decrease the volume of heat that the food is exposed to. This is to avoid partially cooked meat. Because smoke will not penetrate frozen meat in the winter, the smokehouse is frequently heated. Smoke can be made out of a variety of materials. Though hardwood chips such as hickory are popular, bark and corn cobs are also common. Meat can be smoked for up to three weeks before being fully cooked.

Meat can also be kept by salt curing. This method is very useful for preserving fish. This can be accomplished by spreading dry salt into the meat or by brining it. Vegetables can also be preserved with salt or brine. This strategy was originally quite popular in the United States, but it began to fade as the twentieth century progressed.

Fermentation promotes the growth of some particular bacteria. Beneficial microorganisms create chemicals that limit the formation of spoilage-causing microorganisms. Man's intentional fermentation of foods precedes written records and is likely the oldest way of preserving fresh produce. According to research, fermented foods were reportedly eaten in Babylon 7,000 years ago. [1] According to scientists, our forefathers may have found fermentation by mistake and continued to apply it out of desire or necessity. Fermentation preserved foods not just for future use but also made them more edible and tasty. Another benefit of fermenting is the nutritional value gained.

There are various kinds of fermented foods, such as:

- Wine
- Cider
- Tempeh
- Beer

- Miso
- Kimchi
- sauerkraut
- fermented sausage.

Sugar has antibacterial properties as well. Any item containing at least 65 percent sugar is resistant to spoilage. As a result, dried fruit is rarely required for preservation. It merely needs to be dried to the point where sugar makes up 65 percent of its weight. Fruit can be candied or preserved in a syrup, as in marmalades and preserves, or stored in sugar in its full state, as in candied fruit.

# FOOD SAFETY

Food safety relates to how food is handled, prepared, and stored to minimize the danger of people falling ill from foodborne diseases.

Food safety is a worldwide topic that affects a wide range of aspects of daily living. Food safety concepts attempt to keep food from getting contaminated and resulting in food poisoning.

According to research, one out of every six Americans will become hospitalized from food contamination this year? Food contamination puts 128,000 Americans in the hospital every year, resulting in long medical issues. Taking these easy actions will help protect your household safe from food contamination at home.

❖ **Basic Food Safety Procedures at home**

- Washing and cleaning

Thoroughly wash your hands, countertops, and kitchen utensils after each use.

Hands should be washed for at least 20 seconds in lukewarm soapy water. This should be done both before and after handling food.

Wash your hands regularly, particularly throughout these periods when diseases are most likely to spread:

Prior to, during, and after meal preparation

After touching raw meat, poultry, shellfish, or their fluids, as well as uncooked eggs, wash your hands well.

Before you eat,

After visiting the restroom,

After removing a toddler's nappies or cleaning up a messed-up child,

After coming into contact with an animal, animal feed, or animal waste, wash your hands thoroughly.

After coming into contact with dirt

Before and after caring for a sick person

Before and after an open wound is treated

When you've blown your nose, coughed, or sneezed,

After working with pet food or treats.

Forks, spoons, chopping boards, dishes, knives, and countertops should all be washed in warm soapy water. After you've finished handling each food item, repeat the process.

Fruits and vegetables should be rinsed.

Meat, poultry, fish, and eggs should not be washed. When water spills from the sink during the washing phase, bacteria might spread.

Before opening canned foods, clean the lids.

"Pre-washed" labelled products do not require additional washing.

- Keep raw foods separate.

Germs can be transmitted from one food to the next. Raw meat, chicken, fish, and eggs should be kept apart from other foodstuffs. This may be done in your grocery basket, containers, and refrigerator. Except you bring fresh marinades to heat first, don't utilize them.

Keep uncooked meat, poultry, and seafood in airtight containers or leak-proof plastic sacks at home. If you aren't going to use them within a couple of days, put them in the freezer.

Put eggs in their respective cartons in the fridge and place them in the inner section, not the door.

Chop raw foodstuffs on a separate chopping board or plate. Utilize one cutting board for raw meat, chicken, or fish, and separate one for other items that won't be processed before being eaten. When they become damaged, change them.

Cooked and uncooked meals should be served on different plates with different utensils.

- Cooked foods must be able to reach and maintain a high temperature.

Germs are killed by heat.

Cook to safe temperatures:

145°F for Beef, Pork, and Lamb

145°F for fish

160°F for Ground Beef, Pork, and Lamb
165°F for Turkey, Chicken, and Duck
Ensure the food is cooked by using a food thermometer. It's not always possible to know just by looking.

- Chilling

The 2-Hour Rule states that meals should be refrigerated or frozen within 2 hours of being cooked or purchased from the shop. If it's 90 ° or higher outside, do this in one hour.

Food should never be defrosted by merely removing it from the refrigerator. Defrost the food:

In the fridge

Under chilly water

Microwave oven

# METHOD OF MEAT PRESERVATION

## FREEZING

It's impossible to go wrong with freezing, except you utilize the unsuitable container or fail to turn on the freezer. Whether you buy meat in large, hunt it, or raise it locally, portioning the cuts and wrapping them in a freezer sheet or using freezer-safe bags or containers requires no effort. Based on the cut and fat concentration, meat kept at 0° F will last longer, but the flavor will deteriorate after four months to a year. When stored in vacuum-sealed containers, the storage life can be doubled or tripled. To avoid freezer damage, eliminate as much air as possible when using freezer sheets or plastic bags. To save storage, stack meat before it freezes.

Freezing has drawbacks. And the drawbacks might be terrible because when it fails, everything fails at the same time. When the electricity goes off, or your appliance fails, you may not notice until brown-reddish fluid oozes from the inside and blowflies swarm near the source of the foul stench. Many homesteaders have found out the hard way that relying only on a freezer is dangerous. Examine your appliances regularly to make sure they're fully functional. If the door isn't opened, food in a fully loaded freezer can stay frozen for up to a week, giving you enough time to contact a repair service or rescue the food.

## FREEZE DRYING

Freeze-dried foods are one of the greatest survival foods, and they may be organized into single meals that fit within a jar, ready to be hydrated and cooked. The most convenient way to use this meat preservation technique is to get a freeze-drying device that takes care of most of the work for you.

Place fresh or prepared meats on the unit's trays by slicing them. The temperature is then dropped to -30° to -50°F, creating a vacuum around the meat. In this vacuum condition, the meat is slowly heated, and all of the liquid in the meat is converted to water vapor and sucked off.

If you don't want to spend extra cash on a freeze-drying machine, you can freeze-dry using a deep freeze, dry ice, or a vacuum chamber. Some of these procedures can take up to a week and risk freezer damage, resulting in foods that can be dried and kept in pantries.

## DEHYDRATING

Drying meat on smooth rocks in the sun, handcrafted hanging racks, and using electrical equipment is one of the ancient meat preservation techniques. However, a dehydrator can be acquired for less than $40 new or considerably less if bought used. Jerky is dried meat that has been steeped in brine and seasonings before being dehydrated. When mastering how to cook venison, it's common also to learn to create jerky.

Because residual fat can rapidly turn sour and destroy the whole food, dehydrate the thinnest slices of meat and extract it. Slice finely for faster processing; freezing the cuts ahead of time will help you get the thinnest slices possible. If you're making jerky, soak it for up to 24 hours in acid fluids like vinegar, honey, or beer, along with your selected spices.

To maintain safety, University cooperative extensions recommend pre-cooking meat before dehydrating it. Boil for at least 10 minutes in a preheated oven at 275°F or steam/roast to an internal temperature of 160°F. Preheat the oven to 165 degrees Fahrenheit. Place the meat in a straight line on the racks of a food dehydrator and dry at the highest level. Make sure the internal temperature is atleast145 degrees Fahrenheit. Allow four to six hours for drying before storing in sealed containers.

Although frozen meat usually lasts a year, pairing it with dehydration can extend its storage life to several years. It also helps to preserve space. Just dry your meat as directed above, vacuum seals it, and freeze it.

## CURING

Nitrates have recently earned a poor rap. This is partly because huge amounts of sodium nitrate are hazardous. It is, nevertheless, required for curing meat because salt does not eradicate the risk of botulism, whereas sodium nitrate does. To apply this meat preservation approach, look for "curing salts." Due to the additional dye, these are referred to as "pink salts," however they are not similar to Himalayan pink salt.

Dry-curing entails mixing the curing salts with table salt and spices, dry-rubbing meat like pig belly to maintain even covering, and storing in the refrigerator for up to a week. The meat is then carefully cleaned, wrapped in cheesecloth to put pests at bay, and stored for up to eight weeks in a cool, dry area such as a walk-in refrigerator.

Combine a brine with water, table salt, curing salt, spices, and optionally brown sugar to wet-cure meat. For every two pounds of meat, the meat is brined for a day. For large hams, this can take up to a week. Strain the meat on a mesh screen for a day after carefully cleaning it, then store it for up to a month. After smoking, a cured ham becomes much tastier.

## ON THE HOOF

Have you ever pondered why beef, pork, or venison are the most common classical cured or dried meats? Chicken and rabbit sausages do exist, but they are more uncommon. This is because curing and drying were required for bigger animals.

The simplest way of meat preservation is to feed the animal alive till it is consumed. Rabbits, chickens, and geese can sustain a family for one supper and reach butcher size in a matter of months. "Fat calves" were kept for important events when a large group of neighbors or family could share the animal, and hardly anything went to waste. In the parable of the Prodigal Son, the father requested the bigger calf to be butchered to celebrate his son's return.

Families who live off the grid may not have the resources to operate multiple freezers to preserve their animals until they are needed. The difficulty of discovering alternate meat preservation methods for cattle or pigs is avoided by raising smaller, more sustainable animals. Smaller animals also enable homesteaders to grow more meat without requiring much land.

If all grownups have a full-time job, raising animals "on the hoof" may not be possible. It takes effort to butcher, prepare, and brine meat.

If power and appliances are more restricted than food or grass, raising the animals alive for a longer period may solve a storage space challenge.

# HISTORY OF CANNING

Until the advent of canning in the 18th century, the ancient means of food preservation remained unquestioned. Nicolas Appert of France invented the technique between 1795 and 1809. In answer to Emperor Napoleon Bonaparte's request for the development of a new technique of food preservation to serve the troops, he began his experiment. In 1810, Appert presented his findings, for which he was awarded a prize of 12,000 francs.

Appert discovered the technique through a number of careful testing, but he never really comprehended why canning was successful. He had no means of understanding that he was controlling rotting by killing the microorganisms in the food and restricting the entrance of fresh organisms by closing the jars because the germ hypothesis had not yet been created. Instead, he believed that spoilage was caused solely by air and that heating the air in the jars kept it safe. The ultimate elimination of microbes in food was a completely new strategy to food preservation, allowing for the indefinite storage of food.

Appert initially preserved food by storing it in bottles that were heated in a kettle of boiling water. Later on, he explored with pressure cookers. Canned veggies were once a delicacy among the elite, available only in the most expensive Parisian restaurants. Commercial canning, on the other hand, began around 1830. Metal cans, rather than glass, were adopted to save money and lessen the risk of breaking during transportation. Although the food was being canned in the United States in the 19th century, it was the necessity for canned foods to serve troops in the Civil War that primarily enhanced its utilization. Returning troops recognized the usefulness of this approach of preserving food, which, unlike many similar methods at the time, required no specific storage.

Many home canners did not use Appert's full sealed container technique during the nineteenth century. Instead, they employed the "open kettle" method. The meal is submerged in liquid and boiled in this method. The mixture is then swiftly placed in hot jars that have just been heated. The jars are then swiftly covered with lids. To eradicate much of the spoilage-causing organisms, canners in the southern United States cooked the food for shorter periods on three consecutive days. The open kettle approach performed well for foods with a strong acidic nature, such as tomatoes, pear, rhubarb, and peaches.

However, open kettle canning often destroys the fruits or vegetables and increases the risk of spoiling.

Two innovations were required to introduce the more efficient can-cooked process for domestic use. The first was the development of low-cost pressure cookers that made this approach economically accessible. However, without the actions of agricultural extension agencies, this innovation would not have been accessible to the general public.

In 1905, the Louisiana Experiment Station made one of the earliest attempts to distribute this knowledge. Home canning methods were taught by a variety of state extension bureaus in the preceding years, resulting in broad acceptability by the outbreak of the First World War. The increased demand for food during the war only contributed to expanding the adoption of canning.

Canning, however time-consuming, showed to be a far more diverse process than any before used. Teaching canning skills in high school home economics classrooms became common in the subsequent decades. Canning only faced competitiveness in the home food preservation market after the broad usage of freezers.

Like other food-related activities, canning eventually evolved into a competitive activity at county fairs. Frequently, the prizes awarded are sets of canning jars offered by the canning industry themselves.

Agricultural extension services usually recommend metal cans for use in the house, but they are rarely competitive. This is because the containers are barely opened during the contest; doing so would cause the food to spoil. Furthermore, after being taken from the container, many canned foods must be cooked or processed. As a result, tasting the uncooked components would only tell a few questions regarding the food's quality. As a result, contests are frequently judged on how well the food is presented in the glass jars. The color and form of the food, its arrangement in the jar, and the existence or lack of fragments are all employed as indicators. To the uninformed, these may appear to be insignificant or superficial considerations, yet they are directly linked to the economy and performance of home canning.

# BENEFITS OF CANNING MEATS

You'll be pleased to begin storing meat this manner after discovering how to can or bottle fresh meats. Despite possessing all of the necessary tools (pressure canner, jars, rings, etc.) and hearing my pals talk about quick meal prep by grabbing a jar of previously cooked and ready-to-go meat, I was scared by this for many years.

**Save room in the freezer.**

Most individuals don't have a lot of freezer room, and frozen meat occupies most of it. If we can move those meats out of that valuable area and into a canning jar on the table or shelf, we could use that space for stuff like ice cream. Avoiding the cost of spoiled meat in the event of a power failure is just as crucial. Meat is no longer fit to consume if the freezer level reaches the dangerous level of 41 degrees Fahrenheit for two hours more. Everything in your freezer, including ground beef, pork, chicken, brisket, will have to be thrown out. You don't have to bother about power failures if you can some portion of that meat and keep it at room temperature. The fact is, there are so many benefits to canning meat that it's worthwhile getting over your fear and diving in.

**Ability to Purchase in large quantities.**

When we come across a great 'can't-miss' price on meat, we can take the opportunity of it by home-canning it. When you buy several types of meat at a discount and can them, you and your household won't have to consume the same meats over and over by getting them out of the freezer before they go bad.

**Prevent spoilage in emergencies**

We have fuel in our ordinary, non-emergency life. We use it to prepare food, heat, and cool, and we don't give it a second thought. Many folks have a backup plan in case of a power failure, figuring they'll just bring out the camp stove and gas, then prepare or home can all of the meat in the freezer. Everyone has a plan till they get hit in the gut by a power failure- Mike Tyson!

I'm glad to inform you that if you're in the middle of a long term situation, you'll have a lot more to stress about than canning your defrost meats. Why not take charge of it now, while you have the time?

**You're aware of the contents of the bottle.**

There are no secret additives when you can meat at yourself. You are sure of what goes in and out.

Would you like to reduce your sodium intake?
Then leave out any salt or sodium-rich condiments.
Is there anyone in the family who has a food
allergy? When you can meat, you can avoid adding
those additives.

**Meal preparation during a power outage is
painless and straightforward.**

With home-canned meats, cooking during a power
failure is simple. They're already fully cooked and
healthy to consume, so all we have to do now is
add them to any recipe we're making and heat it.
There are no long cooking durations, which waste
valuable alternative fuels. Another alternative is to
rinse the meat and utilize it in a simple household
meal like chicken salad.

helps you save money

The cost of canned meats at the food shop might be
pretty high. A tiny tuna-sized can of chicken (10
ounces) costs roughly $3 where I stay. Getting
canned meats for my big household gets expensive,
but I can bottle an entire quart (2 lbs.) of chicken
for roughly $3.00. I purchase chicken in quantity
for under $2 per pound and occasionally even less.

**Satisfaction**

In a society where practically anything can be
outsourced, there is much to be said about the
satisfaction of doing things yourself. Whenever you
add new talent to your repertoire, your self-reliance

grows. Even better, you may now transfer your knowledge and skills to the subsequent generation. Our primary responsibility is to provide for our families, and doing so well is a beautiful thing.

**There will be less waste.**

Jars for canning exist in a variety of sizes. Use the portion size that your household will consume in a single meal. We use either quarts and pints for chicken and beef at my home since occasionally the supper is for the whole family. On other occasions, the kids are out enjoying kid activities, and its just mommy and daddy and the baby at home.

**Protect the environment.**

We're not saving the environment, but because canning jars are reusable, we're not adding to the waste by using cans. If you purchase new can and lids when you start house canning meat, it will be an investment, but they may also be acquired through yard sales, thrift stores, or simply asking about your area. You might be able to discover an old friend who is willing to give their jars to those who will need them.

Save time

Thanks to the properly prepared meats from home canning, we've saved a lot of time on dinner prep. Although canning the meats takes time at first, it is a targeted and productive amount of work

scheduled for the day. I would open a can of
prepared chicken or ground beef at suppertime,
which makes meal prep so much simpler and faster.
Since we're on the subject of canning and time
saving, one of the simplest products to can is meat.
In most situations, you'll place raw meat in a
canning jar, add some broth or water (depending on
the meat), and pressure can the jars. It doesn't get
any easier than this.

# DRAWBACKS OF THE CANNING METHOD

Although canning has several benefits, it also has some drawbacks. Although the advantages supersede the disadvantages, knowing the weaknesses and risks is important.

- Glass jars are prone to breaking.
- Seals can be damaged, resulting in food spoilage.
- Canning takes a long time.
- When jars refuse to seal, spoilage occurs. However, insufficient preparation or poor hygiene can lead to Clostridium botulinum contamination, which can be fatal. It's always a good idea to strictly follow the directions that came with your canner.
- The majority of canning is made in the summer, which raises air conditioning expenses.
- Canned food does not have the same flavor as fresh food.

- Canned food has a lesser nutrient benefit than fresh food. Freshly harvested mature fruits and vegetables have 65 percent higher vitamins and minerals than canned fruits and vegetables.
- It also necessitates substantial time and financial effort. Using canning tools only once or twice a season may not be sufficient to cover the equipment's expense.
- Canning jars that have been filled are large and weighty. Storage of such jars necessitates the use of heavy-duty shelves. They're also cumbersome to transport from one place to another.

# TOOLS AND EQUIPMENT

## ❖ PRESSURE CANNER

There are numerous pressure canners available. Although most folks prefer the Presto Pressure Canner for amateurs, I found the All American Pressure Canner much simpler to handle and last a lot! It's a little costlier than the Presto, but you'll probably never have to repair anything other than a rubber fitting.

My grandmother gave my mother his All American Pressure Canner, which she has used for another twenty years. My own was a wedding present from her, and it's still running great after fifteen years.

**Significant factors to consider when buying a pressure canner**

- Manufacturers are a major factor to examine when buying a pressure canner.

Pressure canners are made by a variety of companies. Presto and All American are the two most popular brands. They are relatively pricey than water bath canners, but they are incredibly solidly built.

- Budget

The canners you may select are limited by your wallet. Remember that a pressure canner will endure multiple years and can also be used as a water bath canner so that the initial investment will be shared over several years of usage. The price varies from $75 and $500. In general, Presto pressure canners are less costly than similar competitors.

- Capacity

The most typical type (kettle volume) is 16 to 23 quarts, which accommodates seven-quart jars for canning. Fourteen-pint jars can be stored in bigger canners. A pressure canner can pile jars; that is why it can store extra jars per batch than a water bath canner. This is also a compelling argument to go bigger. Because the duration per batch is significantly longer than a water bath canner, that is, between venting, heating, and cooling period, a bigger canner will enable users to can double as many jars in the same amount of time as the smaller designs. You don't have to fill the canner every moment you use it; you can "can" with just one jar or a full load.

A canner that holds at least four-quart jars is the minimum to operate comfortably. It's not advisable to utilize saucepans or pressure cookers with lesser capacity. Pressure cookers that aren't designated as pressure canners should never be utilized for canning since their sides are thinner and could break.

## Overview of some brands and capacity

| Brands | Model | Capacity | Max. no. of pint jars in a single batch | Max. no. of quart jars in a single batch |
|--------|-------|----------|------|------|
| Presto | 1755 | 16 quart | 9 | 4 |
| Presto | 1781 | 23 quart | 19 | 7 |
| All-American | 910 | 10.5 quart | 7 | 4 |
| All-American | 915 | 15.5 quart | 10 | 7 |
| All-American | 921 | 21.5 quart | 19 | 7 |
| All-American | 925 | 25 quart | 19 | 7 |
| All-American | 930 | 30 quart | 19 | 14 |
| All-American | 941 | 41.5 quart | 32 | 19 |

- Dial gauge or pressure weight regulator

After capacity, this is most likely the most crucial factor. There are two kinds of pressure canners: steam canners and pressure canners.

Dial-Pressure Gauge: made by Presto company

Weighted Gauge Regulator: made by All American Pressure Canner

The distinction is in how they control pressure. The weighted Gauge has a weight that raises upward and distributes surplus pressure above the predetermined pressure. A dial pressure gauge pressure canner, on the other hand, permits you to regulate the heat supply to achieve the required pressure.

Weighted gauge canners are superior in every way, except that they are often much costlier. The weighted Gauge is a tiny circle weight or disk positioned on the vent port to regulate inner pressure. Whenever the weighted-gauge pressure canner shakes or jiggles while processing, it releases a small volume of air and steam, they accurately manage pressure. They do not require regular monitoring or accuracy checks throughout processing. The sound of the weight jiggling or bouncing shows that the pressure in the canner is being maintained at the required level.

The dial gauge: is secured to the lid and has a needle to refer to the level of pressure within the canner. Before operating your new dial gauge, make sure it's been tested. Yearly, dial gauges must be verified for precision before usage. When examined at 11 lbs. of pressure, it needs to be changed if your dial gauge displays over or below by more than 2 pounds. Take the expert's advice who tested your canner if the reading is inaccurate by less than 2 lbs.

Over-processing is caused by low results. Modifications can be made to prevent over processing if a gauge is reading less than it ought to be, but they are not required for safety. Under processing is caused by high reading gauges, leading to unhealthy food. Every pound of pressure is needed to attain the canner temperature needed for healthy food production.

## ❖ CANNING JARS

Popularly referred to as mason jars, canning jars are formed particularly for canning.

In 1858, a Philadelphia man called John Landis Mason designed the Mason jar as we currently know. Even when older rivals like Ball and more current competitors like Fillmore hit the industry, the jars were still referred to as Mason jars.

Mason jars are available in a variety of sizes. The choice can be overwhelming at first, but if you consider what you plan to put in the jars and the quantity of that food you would generally use within a suitable length of time after opening a jar, it seems much easier to choose.

They're available in quart (4 cups), pint (2 cups), half-pint (1 cup), and 4 oz. (1/2 cup) sizes. Ball and Kerr are the most popular brands nowadays.

The smallest jars are also called jelly jars, which hold four ounces (one-half cup). Jams, jellies, sauces, and flavored vinegars are among the suggested uses for such jars. They're perfect for preserving liverwurst in our house because one jar carries just needed for four sandwiches. Eight-ounce (one cup) and 12-ounce (one and a half cups) jelly jars are also available. Some brands include a quilted design or another artistic embossing, which makes them appealing as a gift.

Half-pint jars, which are the equivalent of eight-ounce jelly jars but without the ornamental design, are also available. A squat, broad mouth variant of plain half-pint jars is also available, which I don't consider helpful for routine canning.

We use the usual eight-ounce quantity for specialized pickles like pickled beets or pickled green beans, as well as relishes, at our home. We feel that 12-ounce jars are the most convenient size for jams and jellies.

Pint-size Standard and large opening Mason jars are available. The broad mouth jars are much more convenient to load and remove, but the lids are costlier. Almost all of our fruits, veggies, stews, and soups are stored in one-pint jars in our home since that's how much my spouse and I can eat in one sitting. In pint jars, we also store salsa and spaghetti stew.

Mason jars are only available with a wide opening in the pint-and-a-half (three-cup) size. We typically utilize ours to store pickles chopped into sticks, which fit vertically in these jars.

Mason jars with a one-quart (32-ounce) capacity are available with a wide opening or a standard opening. Our wide-mouthed quarts are usually used for canning tomatoes, while our narrower mouth quarts are mainly used for apple juice. Big family homes usually find one-quart jars more appropriate than one-pint jars for canning fruits, veggies, sauces, and soups.

Half-gallon (64 ounces) Mason jars are used for canning acidic liquids. The wide-mouthed variant is now accessible; however, street sales and thrift stores may still have standard half-gallon jars.

Canning jars are divided into two types based on the width of the opening. A small-mouthed jar, often called a regular or ordinary jar, has a 2-3/8-inch opening. A wide-mouth jar has a 3-inch diameter opening.

Because canning jar lids are mainly available in two sizes, the first thing to look for when choosing jars for canning is that their openings are one of these two sizes. The next thing to think about is what foods you'll be canning because the technique of preparing a particular food dictates the type of jars that are suited to some level.

Any canning dish may be made with either style of mouth; the primary distinction is how simple it is to move food into and out of the jar. I prefer to use wide opening jars when canning big chunks of fruit, such as peach halves since they pass easily through the opening. Nevertheless, the type I choose the majority of the time is determined by what I have available.

Canning jars are readily available at various food stores, hardware stores, and big-box retailers. I like to source for canning jars in secondhand stores because they're relatively easy to come by, though you'll have to be patient in growing up your supplies.

## ❖ Recycled Jars

Many goods available at the supermarket existed in glass jars that suited one of two sizes of canning lids when I originally commenced canning on my own. I preserved grape juice from our orchards in a number of one-quart mayonnaise jars that I reused. A colleague who consumed a lot of jarred oysters kept me stocked in a sized jar that I discovered ideal for storing tomatoes.

Other items used to arrive in jars with wide or regular lids, and they still do. These jars may be inexpensive or even free, but they are not suitable for canning.

For one aspect, the top edge is typically narrower and may be rounded instead of being flat, leaving less surface area for a lid to lock firmly on. Furthermore, recycled jars may not be as well tempered as Mason jars, and as a result, they are much more likely to break, particularly when used for preserving veggies or meats that need pressure cooking. Who likes to plant, select, wash, and chop a canner load of green beans just to have a pot full of beans lying in shattered glass?

So, as my canning talents grew, I purchased Mason jars to try my shot at pressure canning. I threw out the recycled jars in preference of the more adaptable Mason jars as my stockpile increased, which can be utilized for any canning procedure.

## ❖ CANNING LIDS

canning lids come in two sections. A rim and a lid. Are you aware that you shouldn't keep the rims on your jars once they've been sealed? After a period, they may begin to rust.

Jars and rims can be reused, but a fresh lid should be used each time you can food. Replacement lids are available with or without additional rims.

## ❖ JAR LIFTER

Although this isn't really a "necessary equipment," it does make the procedure simpler and safer. It usually costs less than \$3. The jars get quite hot when sterilized in a hot water bath or pressure cooked with water transformed to vapor, and therefore demand a method to take them from the cooker. A standard stainless steel jar lifter resembles a pair of large tongs and is specifically built to perform various roles with highly hot jars. The jar lifter's handles are protected with heat-resistant plastic to safeguard hands far from the metal in the instance that the lifter absorbs too much heat.

The tongs grip firmly around the opening of the jar if it is vertically positioned for boiling or sterilizing and over the body of the jar if it is resting horizontally, thanks to the design of the lifter. If the jars are lying flat to be sterilized in a hot water bath, the tongs can also fit within the jar opening or round the body. Jar lifts are ideal for canning and are correctly designed to meet the demands of everyone who can food at home.

## ❖ DUTCH OVEN OR LARGE STOCKPOT

This is where you'll cook the food you'll be canning. A stockpot is a long, straight-sided cooking pot with a flat base. It is comprised of a lightweight material that helps to absorb heat. During the cooking stage, a stockpot includes a lid that allows certain steam to leave. Over time, the sauce's fluid content can be reduced by simmering it in the stockpot. This allows the key tastes to shine through. A stockpot is one of the first culinary tools to prepare vegetables.

The Dutch oven is a thick saucepan constructed with cast iron. It has a strong cast iron cover and sloped edges. The Dutch oven is made to keep moisture in soups and soups and can also be used as a slow cooker. The thicker parts of the Dutch oven ensure that heat is distributed evenly during the cooking phase. The Dutch oven can be used as a camp pot over an open campfire. The pot's cast iron construction allows it to rest in hot coals and even have coals placed on the lid to produce an oven-like atmosphere on a campfire.

In the 1800s, cowboys utilized Dutch ovens on their ride trails and in cowboy campsites. The crock-pot was created as a result of the Dutch oven. It's a slow-cooking Dutch oven that's powered by electricity. The glazing aspect of the Dutch oven makes it ideal for marinating, which can be done with either wine or vinegar. A Dutch oven can boil, cook, braise, and sear food. It can be used as a steamer and can even be stored in the refrigerator to chill down.

## ❖ A STIR STICK OR CHOPSTICK

To remove little air bubbles while closing your loaded jars, slide the little instrument down the interior corners of the jar.

## ❖ A KITCHEN TIMER

A culinary device used to record cooking or meal prep time in units of time. Timers can be either automatic or self-monitored. Electric, battery or spring mechanisms power automated timers, which typically include a dial or digital indication that can be set and signals the lapse of time with a beep or bell. Self-contained timers are designed to measure only a specified amount of time, such as one, two, or three minutes. A self-monitored timer may use noticeable color changes or sand particles to signify that a particular time has passed.

## ❖ Some other tools needed for meat canning includes

- Wooden spoon
- Mixing bowls
- Sharp knives
- Clean towels
- Slotted spoons
- Strainer
- Ladle: to move your food into the jars.

# SOME CANNING PRINCIPLES

## ❖ Venting process

Since at least 1944, the advice for venting has been stated. According to Dr Elizabeth Andress, the USDA in 1944 has advised that pressure canners be vented for 10 minutes before being pressurized. A combination of air and steam will produce gauge pressure without the required high temperature, resulting in under sterilization.

The process for venting was specified in the original USDA Complete Guide, published in 1988. according to a Pennsylvania extension agent, if you're using a pressure canner, make sure to follow the latest suggestion of venting it for ten minutes before enabling the pressure to rise. Allowing steam to flow freely from the canner is referred to as venting.

The canner is "exhausted" once it has been vented. It's a method of allowing steam to escape from your canner for a duration of time before sealing it and bringing it up to pressure. Up to 30% of the sterilizing benefit of a 20-minute operation might be lost without appropriate venting.

A steam vent is found in every pressure canner. When you place your jars in your pressure canner and start the pressure canning procedure, there's a lot of air within the canner that has to leave before pressure can rise.

We removed the weight from the steam vent and let the steam go to accomplish this. Set up a timer for ten minutes after the steam starts to pour out of the vent before putting your weight and letting the pressure rise.

How it occurs:

when water is boiling in a canner with the lid on, the free spaces in the canners becomes filled with a mix of air and steam.

Air is produced from the jars as they boil and inside the canner when the lid is closed.

This steam/air combination will not become as hot as a 100% steam environment, which is a problem because USDA process timeframes are designed for a 100% steam environment alone.

To produce a clean steam atmosphere, we must allow the steam to force all of the air out.

Before pressure processing, steam must pass easily from the opened vent port in the lid for 10 minutes.

## ❖ Elevation adjustment

This is essential, and it all stems from the notion that water boils at a varying temperature depending on elevation. To compensate for the decreased temperature (when you live at a high elevation), we must ensure that the meat in our pressure canner reaches a temperature of 240-250 degrees Fahrenheit to be safe to stay on the table for years.

Luckily, you aren't required to add any extra duration to compensate for elevation when pressure canning, but you will have to apply greater pressure. Because weighted gauges only come in 5-pound intervals, you must put more pressure in blocks of 5 pounds. If you're operating a pressure canner with a dial gauge, ensure you inspect it yearly (including the first time you use it after purchase).

You can change your pressure in smaller amounts if you have a dial gauge.

It's important to note that all pressure canning recipes are developed for a temperature range of 0 to 1,000 feet elevation. As a result, make the necessary adjustments depending on your elevation.

How to find your elevation?

What if you have zero ideas what your elevation is? veloroutes.com allows you to determine your elevation by entering your location.

An alternative approach is to check for "your city, your state, altitude". The first search in my instance was a page that contained my town's elevation.

Calling your county extension office is another viable solution. They might be able to provide you with some valuable details. If your town's department isn't provided, look for the next nearby office.

If you reside in a mountainous environment, be cautious of elevation variations.

PRESSURE CANNING ALTITUDE AND PRESSURE FOR CANNING MEAT

| Altitude in feet | Weighted gauge (lb.) | Dial gauge (lb.) |
|---|---|---|
| 0 - 1000 | 10 | 11 |
| 1001 - 2000 | 15 | 11 |
| 2001-3000 | 15 | 12 |
| 3001-4000 | 15 | 13 |
| 4001-5000 | 15 | 14 |
| 5001-6000 | 15 | 15 |

## ❖ PREVENTING PRESSURE CANNER FROM EXPLOSION

This is a fantastic topic because it appears that everyone in their household has a tale about a pressure canner exploding. The beautiful news about present pressure canners is that they have many precautionary features to keep them from exploding. You'll want to keep an eye out for two factors:

Ensure your pressure canner includes security valves that will release if too much pressure rises.

Help ensure your vent pipe is free of meal crumbs and tidy. To do so, just take the weight and bring your lid up to the light, checking for light through the vent pipe. If you can't, it implies something is obstructing the vent, so you need to clean it before continuing.

# CANNING SAFETY AND PRECAUTIONS

## ❖ SOME USEFUL TIPS FOR BEGINNERS

Before you begin, gather all of your equipment and supplies. It's awful to learn midway through a process that you're out of some ingredients (has happened to me before) or that you can't locate your jar lifter when the jars are set to be removed.

Give yourself plenty of time! Canning is a delightful pastime, but it is unquestionably time-consuming. When you're in a hurry, the fun fades rapidly, and the situation becomes increasingly unpleasant. I have a basic policy that I don't can on weeknights; I leave it for the weekend when I have more free time. The first error individuals commit while pressure canning is altering the recipe. This is one case when you should adhere to the recipe as precisely as possible and only apply recommended canning recipes for preservation. Don't tamper with science; there's a huge science behind ensuring adequate acidity in the food to prevent bacteria from ruining it. Ensure you're following food-safe procedures to ensure you're staying within the right pH and consistency standards for the item you're canning.

Do it with a mate! Washing, drying, and cutting meat, as well as boiling and canning it, is a lot of effort. When you have company, time passes more quickly.

Learn from another who has more expertise than you if you have the opportunity. My grandmother showed me how to can, and asking questions when you're a novice to something is quite beneficial.

The next pressure canning blunder is overfilling the canner. Regardless of how many containers you're canning, don't ever load your pressure canner with far higher above two inches of water from the base. Water bath canning, on the other hand, necessitates submerging the jars. When pressure canning, your containers should never be filled with water up to the necks, and worst of all, covering their lids.

Overlooking headspaces requirements: There's a purpose why different types of canning require different amounts of headspace.

The headspace (or open space) guidelines are in place to guarantee that your food is properly sealed. In order for the jar to be properly sealed, many recipes need at minimum one-inch headspace at the top.

Another common error made by beginners is speeding up the procedure by cooling or releasing pressure very soon. It requires a lot of time for the canner to cool down to room pressure when your processing time is over, so you'll have to wait a little while before you can remove your jars.

This is an important step in the canning technique, so don't rush it by pressing the jiggler, bringing out the weight, or submerging the whole canner in ice water.

Placing your pressure canner in water changes the pressure too rapidly, which can damage your seals, shatter your jars, or even destroy your pressure canner.

## ❖ How to Properly Clean & Sanitize Canning Jars

There are several safety considerations to follow if you plan on canning your meats. Washing and sterilizing your canning jars thoroughly is an essential step. Improperly conducting these steps or utilizing non-safe cleaning products—can lead to serious health issues. Cleaning products that are free of harsh chemicals are considered safe. Safe detergents will not contaminate your canning jars and food.

**Materials for cleaning and sanitizing canning jars**

You will require the following materials to successfully clean and sanitize your jars. Some of them are almost certainly present in your kitchen.

Basin or bucket
Dishwashing liquid
tongs
vinegar (white)
Fresh dish towels
cloths for cleaning
Pressure canner

## CLEANING

You should properly wash and clean your canning jars before sterilizing them. If they've remained resting on a dusty rack without their lids, you'll need to use a clean cloth to remove any dust and dirt.

Dip your jars in a bucket or basin full of heated water and white vinegar if they have scaling or hard-water film on them. For every gallon of hot water, add one cup of white vinegar. Leave the jars to rest in this solution for a few hours before commencing the cleaning procedure.

You could wash your canning jars manually or put them in the dishwasher. In any case, ensure all soap residue is removed. Any food item you want to can be ruined by leftover soap, causing an unpleasant taste.

## STERILIZING

Just like meat you can, the jars and lids may carry bacteria that might thrive and destroy your meat. As a result, all canning tools must be adequately sterilized.

According to experts, sterilization is only required for water bath canning less than ten minutes. If your recipe requires a 10-minute or lengthier preparation period, the jars and lids will be disinfected along with your food.

The best technique to sanitize jars and lids for pressure canning is to use the canning method itself. It's necessary, to begin with, to clean jars and lids; however, the extra sterilizing step can be skipped.

If you want to sterilize jars, the National Center for Home Food Preservation recommends doing so as follows:

Set the washed jars right-side-up on a stand in a canner and load the jars and canner with water to one inch over the tops of the jars. Bring the water to a boil and then boil for 10 minutes at altitudes under 1,000 feet elevation. For every 1,000 feet, you gain in elevation, add one minute. Retrieve the jars one by one when you're set to load them, pouring the water back into the canner. This will leave the canner hot enough to process filled jars.

**Cleaning Your Canning Jars' Lids and Screw Bands**

Would you also need to sanitize the lids and screw bands on the canning jars? No, but give attention to this crucial caution. The lids, made of metal and rubber, are not reusable, contrary to popular assumptions. Each moment you can food, they should be changed.

Because the screw bands are never in contact with the food, they do not have to be renewed. Instead, hand-wash them with heated water and little droplets of liquid dish soap.

After washing screw bands, the first crucial thing is to ensure they are totally dry. Use a dry cotton kitchen napkin for this, then turn it upside down on an additional clean kitchen napkin for a few hours before using it. This will aid to avoid rusting on the bands.

**Jars should be tested for proper seal.**

After cooling for 12 to 24 hours, the jars must be checked for satisfactory sealing before being kept. Loosen the screw bands and inspect the seal using one of the procedures below.

Using a finger or thumb, apply pressure at the middle of the lid. The lid is correctly sealed if it does not shift down or up.

Take the jar by the lid and lift it. The container is correctly closed if the lid stays on without releasing. When verifying the seal, place a hand underneath the jar to hold it if it loosens from the lid, or put it over a table lined with a napkin for padding.

Picking up the jar and looking at the lid at eye level is an alternative to verify the sealing. The jar has correctly sealed if the lid is somewhat bent downwards in the middle.

Test the seal by knocking the middle of the lid with the base of a tablespoon. If it generates a high-pitched ring tone, the jar is fully sealed. If it creates a low bang, the jar may not be well sealed, or there could be stuff at the top of the jar meeting the lid. Pick the jar and inspect the top to see whether there is any food in contact with the lid. If it is, you should use one of the alternative strategies to test for a clean seal.

If any jars are not securely sealed, they can be modified to seal them. Loosen the lid and inspect the rim of the jar for scratches if needed. If the jar has a tear, transfer the substance to a clean jar and make a new lid to sit on top. Reprocess in the same manner as before. Reprocessing will result in an output of lower quality than the initial processed result.

If you don't want to go through the whole procedure for only one or two jars, the unopened jars can be refrigerated and used within two to three days.

**Care and storage of the pressure canner**

Wash the rack and canner inside and out. Dry completely and lay torn newspaper or paper sheets in the pot's base to retain moisture during storage. Insert the rack into the canner.

While washing the canner lid, take special caution to avoid denting or bending it. To clean the gasket, remove it. Carefully dry the lid and gasket. Look for any evidence of damage to the gasket. Change the gasket if it is cracked or damaged.

Because the dial gauge should never be covered in water, pressure canners with a non-removable cover with a dial gauge must be maintained by cleaning the cover off with a moist towel.

The following season before utilizing the dial gauge, keep a record of getting it examined by the local County Extension Office. Remove safety valves and petcocks if they are detachable to be properly washed and dried. To make sure the vent or petcock is clear of dirt, draw a rope through it.

Turn the cover upside down on the pot and put it in a dry area to store the canner. When storing the canner, do not close the lid. Other canning equipment and tools should be stored in the exact place as the canner so that everything is simple to find when the subsequent canning season commences.

## Pressure Canners - How to Use Them Safely

If the pressure canner possesses a dial gauge, it should be examined for reliability once a year before using it. The gauges can be evaluated at most local County Cooperative Extension offices. If the gauge is inaccurate by more than one pound at 5, 10, or 15 pounds of pressure, it should be changed since it may result in inappropriate processing. Before usage, clean all pieces, such as the vent, safety valve, and lid and canner edges.

## Time for Proper Processing

The meals must be processed for the appropriate amount of time to confirm that all germs have been effectively killed. Make sure to modify processing timeframes if you're in a high-altitude area.

## WHAT ARE THE FACTORS THAT AFFECTS PROCESSING TIME?

- Acid level
- Size of the food cuts
- Jars' original temperature
- Is the meat boneless or has bones?
- Size and structure of the jar
- Viscosity
- how tight is the food is arranged in the jar?
- The temperature the food is being processed

## Inspect for Spoilage

Before utilizing canned goods, make sure they are thoroughly inspected for any signs of rotting. Botulism is caused by Clostridium botulinum, found in damaged canned food. It's a great habit to inspect your canned foods for symptoms of spoiling on a routine basis but double-check them before usage. If the food shows indications of spoilage, it should be discarded correctly.

If you're not certain a food is spoilt, do not try to evaluate spoilage by tasting it; instead, toss it in the trash to be safe. The list of indicators of rotting that should be checked before utilizing canned foods is listed below.

Check to ensure that the jar's lid is securely fastened. The jar has an excellent vacuum seal if the middle of the lid is concave.

Check for new leaks or traces of dried food on the jar coming from the top.

Look for discolored areas. It's a sign of rotting if the content is dark in color. If the meal has a mild discoloration, it might be due to mineral elements, in which case the contents are still good.

It is spoilt if the contents are slippery, shriveled, or hazy in appearance.

If the contents of the jar spill out when it is opened, it should be thrown.

Scan for any indications of mold after opening the jar, which might be whitish, blue, greenish, or black in color. Inspect both the bottom of the lid and the contents of the jar for indications of mold.

Sniff the contents; they should be thrown away if they have an off-putting odor.

**Getting Rid of Spoiled Food**

The jars of food must be appropriately disposed of if it has been confirmed that the canned items have spoiled or are likely to rot. If the jar is still sealed, put it in a disposal bag, securely wrap the bag around the jar, and dispose of it in the ordinary trash. The food should be detoxified before discarding if the jar's seal is damaged, the jar is spilling, or the jar has been unsealed. To detox, follow the instructions outlined below.

Fill a pot with the contents of the jar. If the ingredients are rather thick, add additional water to make it simpler to boil.

Put the lid, jar, screw band (if applicable), and any additional utensil that got into touch with the damaged food in a separate pot. To cover the jar with water, turn it on its side if required. Fill the container with enough water to fill the objects by at least one inch.

Bring the water to a boiling state in both pots—Cook for 30 minutes at a full boil.

Throw the contents of both pots in a thick trash bag and seal it securely when they have finished boiling. Try to get rid of the bag and contents appropriately in the waste.

Scrub the table and any areas connected to the food or jars with warm, soapy water. Any brushes or towels used in the cleaning should be thrown in a thick disposal bag, sealed firmly, and thrown away.

Hands should be washed properly with hot, soapy water.

**Canning Storage**

After testing for a proper seal, wipe off any residue on the jars and lids.

Label the jars with the contents and the date of processing. Apply a label on the jars to write the data on, or write on a piece of masking tape. On the surface of the lid, a black marker may be employed to write the item and date.

Keep the jar in a dry, cool, and dark area. The lids may rust if the region is moist, weakening the seal. The appearance and taste of food will be affected if it is subjected to many light or warm temperatures.

Temperatures should be kept between 50 and 70 degrees Fahrenheit. Cans of food ought to be kept for roughly a year before losing their quality if preserved properly.

**Canning tips in summary:**

For the finest appearance and taste in canned foods, choose a high-quality food clean of blemishes, at peak maturity, and not infected.

When processing food for canning, it's crucial to avoid exposing some foods to too much air because they can have dark colors.

The number of canned products you will consume within a year should be canned to preserve them fresh year after year.

Canning should not be done in commercial jars, such as mayonnaise jars. They are poorly sturdy and will fracture or shatter more often during preparation.

Wash the jars in the dishwasher if the preparation time is greater than 10 minutes. During the processing, they will be sterilized.

If you're using spices to flavor your meal before canning it, tie them in cheesecloth instead of placing them straight into the food. This allows them to be taken out before the canning process begins, preventing the food from being too flavorful or colored due to the spices.

Because dried herbs are harsher than fresh herbs, reduce the amount by about 1/3 if dried.

If you're at a higher elevation, be sure to adjust the processing duration in accordance with the Processing Temperature and Time tables. Water

boils at a reduced temperature at higher elevations, necessitating longer processing time.
Do not fasten screw bands after processing.

# SOME COMMON QUESTIONS ASKED

## ❖ How long can I keep canned food in my home?

We recommend that we date homemade canned foods and use them a year from production as the "best before" date.

That date isn't meant to be a protection date but instead an inventory control date to ensure that your cabinet stock stays in good shape.

Theoretically, the seal on your homemade canned foods should last a lifetime, and the contents ought to be secure as long as the seal is intact. Taste and nutritional value may decrease after around a year on certain products (later on others); thus, professionals recommend using up products before a year and prioritizing utilizing up anything that has already passed the year point. Don't worry; it's good; just move it to the top of the cupboard so it may be utilized before new items — just like any sane individual would do with store-bought packed foods.

## ❖ Is there any difference between a pressure cooker vs a pressure canner?

Before you begin, it is essential to know the difference between a pressure cooker and a pressure canner.

Pressure cookers and pressure canners are not similar, and understanding the differences is vital for food safety. Pressure cookers are generally used to quickly cook, roast and other large portions of meat. They exist in a range of sizes, but the majority hold four quarts or less and resemble huge saucepans. Pressure canners, on their end, are used to preserve low-acid food such as vegetables, meat, and fish in canning jars. They are frequently substantially larger, holding 24 half-pint jars or eight-quart jars.

The most significant disadvantage of using a pressure cooker for canning is its small size. The heat-up and cool-down time within the canner is one of the most crucial and undervalued processes in the canning procedure. Pressure cookers are half to one-third the size of typical pressure canners, resulting in greatly reduced heat-up and cool-down durations. This discrepancy could result in a meat that is under-processed, allowing hazardous botulism spores to remain.

Another way utilizing a pressure cooker as a pressure canner is risky is that most of them lack a way to accurately monitor the degree of pressure exerted to the jars, or the mechanisms are inaccurate. It's critical to understand the pressure within the canner to correctly process canned foods. There is no means to tell for sure if your meat has been processed long sufficiently or with appropriate pressure to neutralize botulinum spores. If there is no indicator or if it is faulty.

## ❖ Can You Water Bath Can Meat?

Water-bath canning, often known as "boiling water bath canning," is a simpler way of preserving homemade jam, pickles, and tomato sauce. You may keep the original taste for a year by heating the jars in boiling water at the conclusion of the procedure. In the summer and fall, gardeners and farm owners' markets are brimming with fruit and vegetables. Water-Bath Canning is a fantastic, low-cost solution to preserve the freshness of fruit for use at any time of the year.

When it comes to canning, water bath canning is generally the first thing that comes to mind, but it isn't appropriate for all foods. Water bath canning is only recommended for foodstuffs with high natural acidities, such as most fruits and tomatoes since it process food at low heat than pressure canning.

In conclusion, our focus question is, can we water bath meat? No. There are no exceptions. A water bath just cannot reach an adequately high temperature to safely store meat.

## ❖ Is it necessary to use a pressure canner to preserve meat?

To can meat, you absolutely must need a pressure canner. Because meat is a low-acid product, a pressure canner is required. The only method to raise the meat to a relatively high temperature for a lengthy period; to ensure safety for food preservation is to use a pressure canner.

Don't let your pressure canner frighten you. I'm sure we've all read tales about older adults accidentally blowing up their pressure cooker in the kitchen while cooking. However, today's pressure canners have several advanced safety features that you'll have plenty of notice before something drastic occurs.

## ❖ Is it Possible to Can Meat without a Pressure Canner?

Many folks think using a pressure canner is required when canning meat; however, this is not the case. All you need is a pressure canner to eliminate all the spores that could be harmful if consumed. These spores are not only microscopic and tasteless, but they are also extremely dangerous. If such spores are ingested, severe sickness and possibly death are potential outcomes. You must use a pressure canner because it is the only way to remove them.

## ❖ When pressure canning meat, how do I determine whether to pack it hot or raw?

Observing a tried and true recipe will inform you when to hot or raw pack your meat, whether it comes to pressure canning. Since there's not as much preparatory effort as with a recipe like beef stew or tomato paste, raw packing chicken and turkey has been one of the simplest pressure canning undertakings for newbies.

Using your pressure canner will boost your courage and allow you to try numerous tasks than you ever imagined.

## ❖ Jar type?

Some individuals claim that straight-sided jars are simpler to deal with when preserving meat. Meatballs and patties, for example, may be ideally packed into straight-sided jars for the convenience of working.

However, there is no necessity or advice for straight-sided versus shouldered jars; it is entirely up to you.

## ❖ What should I put in my pressure canner in terms of water?

Unlike water bath canning, which requires the jars to be entirely buried in 1-2 inches of water, pressure canning does not require the jars' neck or lids to be covered with water.

To begin, fill your pressure canner with two inches of water. After placing your jars, ensure the water level doesn't rise past the jars' necks. If there is excess water, you can always remove some before proceeding with the canning process.

# METHOD OF CANNING MEAT

You can choose **raw** or **hot pack**s, but both will result in pressure canned meat. The raw pack is usually misunderstood as a boil, and the hot pack is commonly mistaken as a pressure canned technique, but this is incorrect!

## ❖ RAW/COLD PACK

Simply inserting raw meat cut in cubes into a safe and sanitized jar is all it takes to pressure can meat with a raw pack. Many of the air bubbles inside the jar are removed by squeezing the meat down to the appropriate headspace. Apply the lid to the jar after cleaning the rim with vinegar-soaked tissue or paper towels. Now, fill your pressure canner with the jars and the appropriate quantity of water, and begin by letting it vent heat for 10 minutes before adding the jar and getting it up to pressure.

When raw packing meat for pressure canning, you'll notice that no extra water is used. It'll make its broth on its own.

Proteins stick to the edge of the jar when using a raw pack, and they must be thoroughly washed away.

Don't raw pack in pint normal mouth-sized jars if you don't have a nice cleaning brush to get deep in. The raw pack technique works well with wide opening pints and quarts. I put raw meat in 8 oz. jelly jars with straight sides and a narrow opening. It's considerably simpler to wash than the bigger jars with rounded shoulders.

According to researches done, some people have concluded that the raw pack method:

Saves you preparation time;

Because the meat shrinks during preparation, your jars may appear to be 25% empty.

During preparation, the meat may emit more surplus fat. Surplus fat may flow to the surface of jars, causing an unattractive appearance and perhaps turning rotten over time. (However, particularly in extra-lean minced beef, you'd be shocked at how much fat there is.)

Some claim that jars containing raw-packed meat are more difficult to wash afterwards.

According to North and South Dakota Extension Services,

"When loading jars with raw meat, don't pack them too tightly. A loose pack is when you fill the jar with air. Using the palm of your hand, carefully tap the base of the jar after putting raw meat in the jar and gripping it with one hand. Set a folded kitchen cloth or pot pad on your countertop and tap the jar strongly on the cloth or pot pad. Keep adding meat and tapping the jar's base until the appropriate head space is achieved. Do not squeeze the meat into the jar too tight."

## ❖ HOT PACK

When packaging meat in jars, everything must be hot, as well as the jars themselves. You'll also have to fill the jar with hot water or broth. When it comes to pressure canning meat, hot-packed meat will maintain its form more when used in a meal.

Meat is fried till it is partially cooked when it is hot packed. It will then be placed in the jar and filled to the required headspace with boiling water—this aids in the preservation of the meat's shape and appearance in the jars. The jars will be considerably easier to wash because no proteins from the meat will attach to them.

Be certain that you have the pressure canner water hot when you bring the hot packed jars of meat to it. According to researches done, some people have concluded that the hot pack method:

Since the meat has shrunk during precooking, you can put so much in the jar;

It offers the possibility to burn or brown the meat, generating flavor buttery flavor on the skin of the meat;

Most don't like the mouthfeel of the hot pack with all meats: they say that with more tender meats such as chicken, browning it first can make it stringy.

Note: There is no alternative when it comes to ground meat of any kind: you must do a hot pack by either sautéing the ground meat first or forming it into patties and sautéing those as well. The reason for this is density: raw ground beef would clump together and inhibit even heat transfer through the jar. The ground meat isn't entirely cooked; it's only sautéed until it doesn't form a dense mass in the jar. It's fine to make patties or meatballs (they allow heat to flow around and between them.)

# PRESSURE CANNING RECIPE

## ❖ CHICKEN

### INGREDIENTS

Chicken (bone-in OR boneless): Before you can your chicken, you can either decide to leave the bones in or remove them. This varies on whether you're using a freshly killed chicken, a store-bought complete chicken, boneless chicken breasts or something else.

If you opt to leave the bones in, you'll need to trim the chicken parts up before canning to ensure that they fit into the jars. There will likely be greater wasted space in the jars if you leave the bones in.

You can produce nice uniformed chicken cubes for the jars if you use store-bought boneless chicken breasts or thighs. It's entirely up to you.

Water or broth

Salt (optional)

### KITCHEN TOOLS

Pressure canner

Canning jars: You have the option of using pints or quarts. If you don't fancy the sight of leftover chicken, pint-sized jars are generally the correct size for one meal. I wouldn't mind utilizing quart jars because it means I'll have chicken available for another meal later that week.

seals, and rings

Sharp knife or kitchen shears

Ladle and bubble tool

Canning funnel, lid lifter, and jar lifter

NOTE: If you're butchering your domestic chickens, ensure they're dressed and chilled for at least 6 hours prior to canning. If you're using store-bought chicken, it's already been prepared and refrigerated and is good to go. Before beginning the canning procedure, ensure the chicken(s) are properly defrosted.

**PROCEDURE**

Get your pressure canner ready.

Get your chicken ready. Cut the meat at the joints to preserve the chicken with bones, and ensure the parts fit into the jars. Boneless chicken should be cut into small parts. If you like, you can take out the skin from your chicken.

- RAW PACK METHOD: Load your jars with chicken chunks loosely, allowing 1 ¼ -inch headspace. If desirable, add ¼ – ½ teaspoon salt on pint jars and ½ –1 teaspoon salt on quart jars.

- HOT PACK METHOD: Briefly cook your meat (you can boil or bake it). Load your jars with slightly cooked chicken and heated chicken broth or water, allowing 1 ¼ inch headspace. If necessary, add ¼ – ½ teaspoon salt to pint jars and ½ –1 teaspoon salt to quart jars.

Using a canning tool or a knife, release air bubbles from jars.

Clean the rims, set the lids/rings, and process in a pressure canner according to the instructions below: Process quarts for 90 minutes and pints for 75 minutes for jars lacking bones (both hot and raw pack processes). Process pints for 65 minutes and quarts for 75 minutes (both hot and raw pack procedures) for jars having bones.

When using a dial gauge pressure canner, it is recommended you process jars at 12 pounds' pressure (altitudes of 2,001 to 4,000 ft.) or 11 pounds' pressure (altitudes of 0 to 2,000 ft.). Process jars at 10 pounds' pressure (altitudes of 0 to 1,000 ft.) or 15 pounds' pressure (altitudes above 1,000 ft.) in a weighted gauge pressure canner.

## ❖ BEEF
### TOOLS AND INGREDIENTS

- Pressure Canner
- Clean Pint or Quart Canning Jars
- Seasonings of your choice (optional)
- Salt (optional)
- Chuck Roast
- Sharp Knife or electric knife
- Fresh canning lids and rings
- Hot water or broth
- Pepper
- Large Bowl
- Cutting board
- Long-handled spoon
- Jar Lifter
-

## HOT PACK PREPARATION

- Chop the chuck roast into ONE INCH cubes to start canning meat (eliminate any too fatty parts).
- Load your jar with raw beef, but don't compress it too firmly. Allow an inch of headspace at the jar's top.
- Sprinkle the meat with salt and pepper, as well as any other spices you like.
- Fill the jar with hot water or broth, allowing a one-inch headspace. Release any air bubbles in your jars with the base of a spoon or similar utensil (carefully move the beef

from one side to the other for air to escape). Using your fingers, carefully secure the lid and ring on the jar.

- Make sure there is no dirt on the rims of your jars by cleaning them down.

- Heat your pressure canner until it's hot, then switch it off and start filling it. Ensure your canner has a rack at the base to keep your jars from cracking. Cover the canner with the lid and seal it. Follow the information for your pressure canner because each is unique.

- While you're starting, be certain there's no jiggler or load on the top of your canner; you want the pressure to develop up and drive the air out.

- Reload the heat and monitor your canner for a continuous heat flow every 5 minutes. Setup the timer for 10 minutes and then sit back and relax. Put your weight or jiggler on top of the canner after the time is up.

- To raise the temperature, use the recommendations that came with your pressure canner. While you're increasing the pressure in your canner, keep a sharp eye on it. Pint jars should be processed for 1 hour 15 minutes, and quart jars should be processed for 1 hour 30 minutes.

- Turn off the heat beneath your canner when they're done and let it cool down gradually. DO NOT Lift THE WEIGHT; instead, wait until the pressure has dropped to zero. Wait 10 minutes after removing your weight.
- Then uncover your canner and set the jars aside to chill for 18 to 24 hours in a draft-free spot.
- Mark and date your jars after they've cooled, then keep away in a dark closet until you're ready to use them. You may also wash the exterior of your jars if needed.

**COLD PACK METHOD**
**INGREDIENTS**
- Raw beef/chunk
- Pepper
- Salt (your choice)
- Seasoning (optional)

**COLD PACK PREPARATION**
If you want to season your beef with salt, put 1/2 tsp per pint jar and 1 tsp per quart jar. Pack each heated jar with meat, allowing a 1-inch headspace. Add no liquid to the batch. Clean the rims, set the lids, and process in a pressure canner.

### ❖ BEEF STEW
**INGREDIENTS FOR QUARTZ JAR:**

- 1 ¼ teaspoon sea salt
- ½ cup of diced onions
- ½ cup of carrot, cut into tiny bits
- 1 cup beef stew meat, cut into 1″ cubes
- 1 cup potatoes, peeled and cut into cubes
- 2 cloves of minced garlic
- ½ teaspoon dried rosemary
- ¾ teaspoon dried thyme
- ¼ teaspoon ground black pepper
- 

## PREPARATION FOR HOT PACK METHOD:

- Brown the beef in a heavy Dutch oven or soup pot with 1 tbsp. Of lard, bacon fat, or coconut oil. It only has to be browned on the top and not completely cooked inside.

- Fill the heavy Dutch oven halfway with water and put the other ingredients. Bring the stew to a boil, then put it into quart-sized jars that are hot and clean. Allow 1-inch headspace.

- Wipe the rims of the jars, set the two-piece lids, and prepare for 1 hour 20 minutes at 10 pounds of pressure in a pressure canner. (Or, if you stay at a high elevation, ensure to adjust to 15 pounds of pressure.)

- Before serving, reheat the beef stew in a pot on the fire for 10 minutes. Taste before dishing and sprinkle with more salt or spices as necessary.

## ❖ PORK

**INGREDIENTS**

PORK: Pork loin is what I prefer. It's even better when it's on offer. I'm referring to the entire loin, not just the tenderloin. Although the tenderloin is delicious, it is too tiny and pricey to store in quantity. The weight of a complete pork loin will range from 5 to 10 pounds. They have minimal fat if they're well-trimmed. It's okay even if there is a large fat deposit; it only adds to the calorie count!

Unlike other parts such as the shoulder or the leg, the loin has little or no bones. The bones are a waste of weight that won't help your canned products. You'll also have to devote more effort to cut them out.

Based on where the pork loin is cut, it has two to three muscles. Only one is found in most center-cut loins. Butchering is made simple and fast as a result of this.

SALT: Table salt and canning salt are very identical. The main distinction is that canning salt does not contain anti-caking chemicals. Anti-caking chemicals are responsible for the hazy canning fluid. It's not a vital issue; rather, it's a matter of taste.

**RAW PACK INGREDIENTS**

Sixteen pounds' pork loin: It's an ease to cut up pork loin. The only requirement is that the sections must be at least 3/4 inches thick. If the cubes are larger than 3/4", the heat and duration will be inadequate to reach the center of the pork. This results in unhealthy canning and a high risk of sickness.

If you're preparing a loin, start by slicing it up. The entire loin was chopped into 3/4-inch rounds. Each slice is then sliced into 3/4-inch cubes. That's all there is to butchering.

4 teaspoons canning salt

## RAW PACK PREPARATION

- In a saucepan, put rings and lids, fill with water, and heat to a boil.
- Fill your canner with water and follow the instructions that came with the canner.
- Pork loin should be cut into 3/4-inch cubes.
- Fill each quart jar with two pounds of cubed pork T. Don't worry about any air holes; the pork's stock will cover them as it cooks. 1" of headroom is required.
- To each jar, add 1/2 teaspoon of canning salt.
- Using a paper napkin soaked with vinegar, wipe the rim clean.
- Place the lids and rings on top. On the jars, place the lids in the middle. Tighten the rings with your fingers.
- Fill the canner with jars.

- Tighten the lid on the canner according to the manufacturer's instructions.
- Increase the heat to high.
- Allow time for the canner to warm up.
- Allow for a strong and constant stream of steam to emerge from the vent. Wait 10 minutes for the canner to vent. Fill the vent with the weight.
- When the weight begins to jiggle, turn up the heat till it jiggles 4-10 times per minute — the temperature should be between 240 and 245 degrees F. (115 F to 118 Celsius).
- Allow 90 minutes – 75 minutes for pint jars – to process in the canner.
- Put off the heat once the procedure is completed.
- Let the temperature in the canner return to 200 ° F. (93 Celsius).
- Allow 10 minutes for the canner to vent after removing the weight.
- Lift the lid first, then the jars.
- Let the jars chill to room temperature. Keep an ear out for the "ping" of the lids sealing.
- Check to see whether the lids have dimpled and are no longer flexing.
- Remove the rings and give the jars a brief rinse after they've cooled.
- Each jar should be labeled and dated.

## ❖ TURKEY

Canning turkey at yourself preserves a bunch of freezer room and enables you to stock your store with readily available, home-cooked dishes. The method is quick and uncomplicated, whether you're preserving leftover turkey after Christmas or raw packing turkey flesh right into canning jars.

### CANNING TURKEY LEFTOVERS

When canning turkey, the flesh is commonly cooked to approximately two-thirds done before being packed into jars. Because turkey is moderate-fat meat, it tends to be dry when fully cooked, and it is frequently overcooked. Nobody wants to give their household salmonella on Christmas, and it's far simpler to smother a dry turkey with gravy or cranberry sauce than to be concerned about overcooked flesh.

If you want to can completely cook leftover turkey, there are a few things you can do to keep the canned turkey from becoming too dry:

Try not to overcook it!

To keep the meat moist while cooking, brine it first.

To add a touch of additional fat to an extremely lean meat, rub butter underneath the skin.

Together with the turkey flesh, sprinkle salt into the canning jars.

Save the thicker, higher fat brown turkey for canning and dish the white meat.

**STEPS**

- Start by removing any residual flesh from the turkey carcass and boiling it in water with onions, garlic, and flavorful spices to produce a tasty turkey bone broth. I let mine simmer for at least 3-6 hours on medium heat and occasionally overnight.

- Depending on your preference, chop the remaining turkey flesh into bits. I slice them into around 1-inch pieces so that they may be served in a variety of ways.

- If you want, you can fill the jars with complete breasts or thighs, bones and everything. Allowing the bone in causes a hassle for later and, in my view, is a waste of jar space. However, the size of the portions is unimportant; it is entirely up to your family's preferences.

- Pre-cooked turkey is no different when it comes to shrinking during the canning process. Although cooked turkey shrinks less than raw meat, it should still be packed securely into canning jars. The idea is to pack as much meat into every jar as possible whilst also providing a healthy 1 1/4-inch headroom at the top.

- Clear air bubbles with a non-metallic utensil after pouring boiled turkey stock over the meat. Examine around the jar's edges for any leftover air bubbles, then press down on the middle of the meat to attempt to push them out.

- There may be meat subjected to air within the canning jars if air bubbles are present after canning. Although it is safe, the flesh will discolor and dry up with time.

- And that's all, start the canning process.

**SHOULD YOU RAW PACK TURKEY?** With or with no bones, Raw turkey flesh can be placed into canning jars. Turkey meat is the only ingredient in the jars, and the flesh will make its liquid throughout the canning operation.

Although raw packing eliminates the additional labor of boiling the turkey and producing turkey stock for packaging, it results in a lower-quality product. Raw turkey frequently lacks sufficient fluid to fill the canning jar with tasty liquid, keeping the flesh exposed to air. You'll also be missing out on the added taste that a well-made bone broth may provide.

I'd still suggest cooking the turkey before packing it into jars for canning, even if you're not canning leftover turkey. A cooked turkey is also much easier to debone, even if it's just slightly cooked before canning.

|  | CANNING BONELESS TURKEY | CANNING BONE-IN TURKEY |
|---|---|---|
| Pint jars | 75 Minutes at 10 lbs. pressure (below 1,000 feet) | 65 Minutes at 10 lbs. pressure (below 1,000 feet) |
| Quart jars | 90 Minutes at 10 lbs. pressure (below 1,000 feet) | 75 Minutes at 10 lbs. pressure (below 1,000 feet) |

**REPEAT TURKEY PROCESS FOR CANNING DUCK, GOOSE, AND GAME BIRDS**

## ❖ RABBIT

In France and the United Kingdom, nutrient-dense rabbit is extremely famous. Its flesh is abundant in B12 and selenium and has a low caloric content compared to its protein content.

**INGREDIENTS AND TOOLS**

- Rabbit {in any quantity}

- Boiling Water
- Canning Salt
- Clean Canning Jars, Lids, & Bands
- Pressure Canner

## PREPARATION

- Soak your rabbit flesh in salt water brine for 30 minutes—one hour for smaller rabbits, six to twelve hours for elderly or wilder rabbits. There are a few motives for this, depending on the sort of rabbit you're working with (wild or domestic):
- The salt will aid in the removal of any blood from the flesh. There is typically not much blood when domesticated rabbits are caught and left to drain completely. Blood in the meat would be a bigger problem with wild rabbits that weren't cleaned right away in the bush. In either case, this procedure will aid in the removal of excess blood from your meat.
- Wild and mature domesticated rabbit meat can be rough and dry. The meat will be tenderized and moistened by salt brine.
- The salt brine, more common in wild games, will help remove the "gamey" flavor from rabbit meat. Domestic rabbit does not have that flavor, in my opinion, but I have read that

it does, so if you are concerned about it, you should salt brine your meat.

- Stuff the meat into heated jars with 1″ headspace once it has been split at the joints. Deboning isn't necessary because the final canned result will practically fall off the bones, but you can do it if you like.

- Gently pour in the heated water, allowing a 1″ headspace this time. Remove retained air bubbles by carefully sliding a non-metallic tool down the interior sides of the jar. Clean the rim and the threads. Close the lid and ring.

- Start the canning process.

## ❖ SEAFOOD

Canned fish is a popular food option. Canned fish is high in protein and several other necessary nutrients, including omega-3 fatty acids, abundant in many varieties.

The catch has landed, and there are many fish to prepare and consume right now. Canning is a common way to preserve seafood. However, it is critical to pack and treat seafood according to the package recommendations to ensure its safety when you open it to consume it.

**PREPARATION**

- Remove the viscera from salmon, trout, steelhead, and other fish (excluding tuna) as soon as possible after a catch and refrigerate until set to preserve.
- Remove all blood, head, tail, and fins while washing and cleaning the fish.
- Cut the fish lengthwise into lengths that will sit in a half-pint or pint jar. One half-pint jar will hold around 1 pound of fish.
- Fill clean canning jars with fish. If desired, flavor with 1-3 teaspoons vegetable oil or French-style dressing per pint. Some individuals may make sure to place the skin side out so that when the fish is removed from the jar, the skin will hold to the jar and be easy to remove.
- Clean the rim of the jar after laying the fish slices in it. Clean the rim with a damp paper napkin. Soak the napkin in vinegar if you're preserving fatty seafood like tuna or salmon. This will assist in removing the fat deposit from the jar's edge.
- Position hot two-piece lids on the jar. Process for 100 minutes at 11 pounds' pressure (dial gauge) or 10 pounds' pressure (weighted Gauge).

**FOR SMOKED FISH:**

Fish has a very low storage life once it has been smoked. The bacteria in smoked salmon can cause botulism food infection even when refrigerated, and after 2-3 weeks of preservation, they may multiply.

Putting smoked salmon in vacuum-sealed containers does not make it safe to consume outside or in the refrigerator. If you want to store fish for more than two weeks after smoking it and vacuum sealing it, make sure you freeze it.

Another alternative is to can. After canning, completely smoked fish that is dry enough to consume will be dry, darkish in color, and have a pronounced smoked taste. Fish that will be canned must be smoked for a shorter period than fish consumed straight away for the greatest quality.

Smoke the fish moderately if you're making canned smoked fish. Only smoke the quantity of fish you'll be able to can in one day. Smoke the fish for up to two hours, based on how strong you want the smoke to taste. Do not taste the fish for doneness because this amount of smoking does not thoroughly cook the fish. The easiest method to determine when it's done is to track the weight—weighing the fish before and after smoking is used to evaluate weight loss. A ten percent weight reduction results in a decent canning product. After canning, a 20-30% weight reduction is likely to make the product excessively dry.

- Transfer the smoked fish into pint jars when set to can. Half-pint jars can be used successfully, although the flavor of the output may be compromised, and the jars will swim in the canner.

- Arrange smoked fish into jars upright, allowing a 1-inch headspace between the fish and the jar's top. Wipe the jar's rim with a moist paper cloth before putting on the two-piece lids.

- Can the jars at 11 pounds' pressure (dial gauge) or 10 pounds' pressure for 110 minutes (weighted gauge canner).

- Assess for indicators of deterioration before using the goods, such as color changes, an off-putting odor, unsealed lids, or oozing liquid when the jar is opened.

## PRESSURE CANNING SHRIMP:

- As soon as the shrimp are captured, remove the heads. Cool on ice until set to pressure can. If you're using frozen shrimp, make sure they're completely defrosted before canning. Wash the shrimp and strain in a colander when set to preserve.

- Make a brine by combining ½ cup canning salt and 1 cup vinegar in a big stockpot for every gallon of water. Bring the water to a boil with the beheaded shrimp for 9 to 10 minutes. Drain the cooked shrimp in a colander and rinse for 3 minutes under cool water. Allow to cool.

- Make a new brine by combining 2 teaspoons of canning salt with 1 gallon of water in a pot. To dissolve the salt, stir thoroughly. Over high temperature, bring to a complete boil.

- Remove the shells from the shrimp and put them into jars with 1 inch of headspace. On the shrimp, pour the boiled salt brine. If you're limiting your sodium consumption, just use boiling water and leave out the salt. Release any air bubbles and, if required, add more brine to keep the 1-inch headspace.

- Wipe the rims of the jars with a warm, damp towel soaked in vinegar—hand-tighten the lid and ring on every jar.

- Fill your pressure canner with boiling water according to the producer's instructions, usually 3 quarts. Put the heated jars in the pressure canner, secure the lid, and raise the pressure canner to a boil over high heat. Allow 10 minutes for the canner to vent. Shut the vent and keep heating until the dial gauge reaches 11 PSI and the weighted Gauge reaches 10 PSI or based on your altitude.

Process both pints and half-pints for 45 minutes.

- When the timer goes off, and the processing is finished, turn off the heat and gradually let the pressure in the canner drop to zero. This might take anything from 30 minutes to an hour. Lift the scanner lid after the pressure in the canner has dropped to 0 PSI, making sure to keep the steam away from your face. Leave the canner to lie uninterrupted for 10 minutes before retrieving the jars.

- Set jars on a work surface and set aside to cool for at least 8 hours or longer. Loosen the rings and wash the jars in lukewarm soap water. Keep rings to reuse, then mark and date each jar before storing.

## PRESSURE CANNING CLAMS:

Either whole or minced:

## PREPARATION:

- Keep the clams alive on ice until they're ready to be canned. Clean and rinse the shells properly, then steam for 5 minutes before opening. Remove the clam flesh. Clam juice should be collected and saved.

- Wash the clam flesh with 1 teaspoon of salt. Boiling water with 2 tablespoons lemon juice or ½ teaspoon citric acid per gallon should be used to rinse and cover the clam flesh—Cook for 2 minutes and then strain.

- Grind clams in a meat blender or food processor to create minced clams. Fill heated jars with pieces, allowing 1-inch headspace and adding hot clam juice and boiled water as required. Release any air bubbles and, if necessary, fix the headspace. Using a wet clean paper towel, clean the rims of the jars—process after adjusting the lids.

Made in the USA
Monee, IL
29 November 2023

47779651R00052